Photography by Will Heap

THE **FESTIVE** FOOD OF

India and Pakistan

BY LOUISE NICHOLSON

Kyle Cathie Limited

First published in Great Britain in 1992 by
Kyle Cathie Limited
122 Arlington Road
London NW1 7HP
general.enquiries@kyle-cathie.com
www.kylecathie.com

ISBN 1 85626 677 X
ISBN (13-digit) 978 1 85626 677 2

pages 4–5: Driver leading his camel through the Thar Desert, Rajastan;
Peter Adams/Taxi/Getty Images
pages 6–7: Shiv Niwas Palace, Udaipur; Panoramic Images/Getty Images

Designed by **pinkstripedesign.com**

Photography by **Will Heap**

Illustrations by **Sally Maltby**

Picture research by **Sharon Tagg**

Home economy by **Annie Nichols & Lizzie Harris**

Styling by **Roisin Nield**

Production by **Sha Huxtable & Alice Holloway**

Louise Nicholson is hereby identified as the author of this work in
accordance with Section 77 of the Copyright, Designs and Patents Act 1988.

A Cataloguing in Publication record for this title is available from the
British Library.
Reproduction by Colourscan
Printed and bound in China by SNP Leefung Printers Limited

**Each recipe serves 6 people. An Indian meal comprises
several dishes, the number depending upon how many are
to be fed, the importance of the occasion and how much time
the cook has.**

CONTENTS

REPUBLIC DAY

A national holiday, 26th January, is one of the few fixed dates in the festival calendar. It marks the day in 1950 when the newly created independent Republic of India was inaugurated and its Constitution came into force. The place to be is the capital, New Delhi, where Sir Edwin Lutyens' city is the backdrop for a spectacular day-long parade.

Crowds from all over India gather in the chilly morning all along Raj Path, the three-mile-long processional route. The President leads the parade in his ceremonial coach, escorted by the President's Body Guard founded by Warren Hastings in 1773. Then follow giant thematic floats representing each state and decorated with flowers, images of gods, and tableaux of locals singing and dancing. Between them come legions of folk dancers and literally hundreds of gaily caparisoned elephants and camels, while above flies a helicopter in full elephant fancy-dress showering rose-petals. Meanwhile the folk-dance festival fills the cultural halls each evening, the government buildings twinkle with miles of fairy lights, and pavement stall holders do a roaring trade.

left and righ Republic Day in New Delhi; Kapoor Balder/Sygma/Corbis

CHAAT

Street snacks are a vital part of Indian life and chaat stalls are found throughout India. The spicy mixture has infinite local varieties but usually includes something fried, some curd, chutney and garnishes, and it is always eaten cold. The renowned Delhi chaats tend to include dry mango and fresh mint and be savoury or fruit based.

Aloo Pooina Chaat

1 teaspoon each of cumin seeds and coriander seeds

6 medium-sized potatoes, boiled in their jackets, peeled and cubed

2 small cucumbers, peeled, seeded and cubed

1 teaspoon salt

2 teaspoons lemon juice

¼ teaspoon each of black and red cayenne pepper

115g chopped fresh mint leaves

1 In a frying pan, quickly dry-roast the cumin and coriander seeds, and then blend until fine.

2 Mix the diced potato and cucumber, tossing in the salt and lemon juice. Add the spices and mint, mixing gently to prevent the potato breaking up.

Dahi Bhalla Chaat

THE MASALA

30g each of cumin seed and black peppercorns
2 teaspoons black cardamom seeds
1 teaspoon green cardamom seeds
2.5cm cinnamon stick
3 teaspoons yellow chilli powder
2 teaspoons black salt powder

1 In a frying pan, quickly dry-roast all the ingredients except the chilli and salt powder. Blend or pound all to a fine powder, combine with the chilli and salt and set aside.

THE SAUNTH (SWEET MANGO CHUTNEY)

3 teaspoons cumin seeds
1 teaspoon each of black salt, black peppercorns and black cardamom
seeds
50g mango powder
250ml water
250g sugar

1 In a frying pan, dry-roast the cumin seeds, then blend or pound finely with the salt, peppercorns and cardamom seeds. Sieve the mango powder and heat in the water, whisking continuously until it thickens to a sauce-like consistency. Add the sugar and spices and cook gently for 5 minutes. Sieve.

THE BHALLAS

300g urad dhal (white split gram bean) without husk
pinch of asafetida
oil for deep-frying

1 Soak the urad dhal for 1 hour. Drain and blend to a fine, fluffy paste (do not add water or it will be too thin). Dissolve the asafetida in a teaspoon of water and add to the paste.

2 In a deep, heavy saucepan, heat some oil to a moderate heat. With wet hands, shape the paste into small balls and carefully drop into the hot oil. Fry until crisp and golden brown. (You can add raisins and nuts before frying, in which case the finished chaat will be called Dahi Gujia.)

TO ASSEMBLE THE DAHI BHALLA CHAAT

You need, in addition to the masala, saunth and bhallas:
500ml yogurt
chilli powder

1 Soak the bhallas in lukewarm water for 30 minutes and then drain and squeeze off moisture.

2 Whisk the yogurt with a little salt.

3 Arrange the bhallas on a plate and sprinkle with chilli powder and chaat masala. Mask with the yogurt, pour some saunth over and sprinkle a little extra chilli powder for decoration.

Id Ul-Fitr

This Muslim festival celebrates the end of Ramadan, the ninth month of the Muslim calendar which, since it is lunar, falls at a different time each year. It was during Ramadan that the Prophet Muhammed received his revelation. To commemorate it, the faithful over the age of twelve do not eat or drink during daylight hours for the whole month, thirty days. As the Qur'an decrees, they must 'strictly observe the fast from dawn until nightfall' and 'be at their devotions in the mosque'.

The moment the sun sets in the Islamic communities of the North-west Frontier Province of Pakistan there is a mad rush to the cafés for *iftari* (breakfast) which may include sizzling kebabs and large bowlfuls of Haleem (grains cooked with meat, page 92) with large parathas and washed down with hot, sweet tea. But the feasting at the end of Ramadan surpasses all and may include roasting a whole goat or lamb stuffed with spices and rice. The Raan of Lamb, easier to fit into a Western oven, is equally popular.

right Taj Mahal, Agra; Harvey Lloyd/Taxi/Getty Images

RAAN OF LAMB

The aroma of spices will be almost intoxicatingly mouth-watering.

1.35–1.8kg leg of lamb
1 tablespoon corn oil
 or clarified butter

THE GARAM MASALA:
5cm cinnamon stick
20 black peppercorns
8 large black cardamom pods
12 cloves
1 teaspoon black cumin seeds

THE MARINADE PASTE:
2 medium heads of garlic (about
 20 cloves), peeled and ground
2.5cm piece of fresh ginger,
 peeled and ground
½ teaspoon red cayenne pepper
1 teaspoon each of ground
 cinnamon, white cumin
 and salt
2 teaspoons yogurt

1 To make the masala, coarsely grind all the ingredients.

2 To make the marinade paste, mix all the ingredients well.

3 Cut any surplus fat from the lamb, and make deep slits all over the meat. Rub in the paste, pushing it deep into the cuts to allow the flavour to penetrate the meat. Rub over the oil, cover and leave for several hours or overnight; the longer the better.

4 Before cooking, scoop up the paste and rub into the meat again, then sprinkle over 1 teaspoon of the garam masala.

5 Seal for 20 minutes in a preheated oven, 230°C/450°F/ gas 8, until brown, then turn down the oven to 190°C/ 375°F/gas 5 for 1 1/2 hours, until it is very well done, turning over once.

6 Remove from the oven, sprinkle with 1 more teaspoon of garam masala to give a fresh aroma, rest it for 15 minutes, then carve.

PULAO

2 medium-sized onions
1 tablespoon vegetable oil

THE YAKHNI (MEAT SOUP):
1 tablespoon vegetable oil
675g shoulder of lamb, cut into
   2.5cm pieces
6 large garlic cloves, peeled
   and crushed
2 tomatoes, chopped
1 teaspoon salt
900g Basmati rice
2 teaspoons salt
1 teaspoon vegetable oil
garam masala (prepared for
   the Raan of Lamb page 17)
½ teaspoon ground black cumin

1 Slice the onions finely and pat dry. In a frying pan, heat the oil and fry the onions on a high heat until deep brown – this caramelising gives the Pulao its distinctive colour. Drain on kitchen paper, then pound to a paste.

2 To make the *yakhni*, heat the oil in a saucepan and fry the meat for 2 minutes. Add the garlic and tomatoes. Stir until the meat is golden brown. Add the salt and stir until the tomatoes are cooked, splashing with a little water to prevent sticking. Add the onion paste and 575ml water, cover and cook over a medium heat until the meat is tender, about 1½ hours. Then raise the heat to reduce the liquid by about a half.

3 Wash the rice and soak it for 10 minutes. In a large saucepan, bring 2.25 litres water to a furious boil. Add the rice and salt and boil for 5 minutes, cooking only until the rice grains are soft at their ends but still hard in the centre. Drain.

4 To assemble, take a large, ovenproof, heavy-bottomed pan and pour in a teaspoon of oil. Using a slotted spoon, lay the rice on the bottom, then all the meat on top of it. Sprinkle with ½ teaspoon of garam masala and 100ml yakhni liquid round the sides so it seeps down to give the traditional brown-and-white, two-colour effect. Sprinkle over another ½ teaspoon of garam masala and the cumin. The pulao should come halfway up the pan.

5 Cover with a tight layer of foil and the lid. Cook on a high heat for 2 minutes, then continue cooking in a preheated oven, 150°C/300°F/gas 2, for 45 minutes. Before serving, give the pan a good shake.

PONGAL

This is the January rice harvest festival of south India, celebrated in particular in Tamil Nadu. Four days of holiday celebrations begin with Bhogi, when spring cleaning and bonfires of old possessions drive evil spirits out of the houses. The women draw exquisite *kolams* (rice paste patterns) on the great rice pot, the stove and the doorstep.

The next day is Pongal itself. Families bath and massage each other and put on new clothes. They then feast on newly harvested rice boiled up with sugar cane, turmeric and other ingredients in the decorated pot. When the froth is *pongu*, 'boiling over', some is offered to Surya, the sun god, and the more it boils over the better the year ahead will be. The next day is Maattu (cattle) Pongal, when the cows and bullocks are lovingly washed, sprinkled with turmeric to ward off evil, anointed with red powder, garlanded and their horns painted bright colours. Then they have their dish of Pongal rice before being paraded round the streets.

right Painting bull at Harvest Festival; Bob Kirst/Corbis

THALI

Thali simply means platter. *Katori* (little pots) containing different dishes are arranged round the edge of the thali in a specific order to balance the flavours. They are eaten with the fingers or teaspoons from left to right, beginning with a pulse, progressing through vegetables to yogurt, then possibly something fried and finally the sweet dish. The steaming boiled rice piled in the centre can be supplemented with breads such as fried puri. The number of *katoris* varies from the basic four – a pulse, vegetable, yogurt and sweet – right up to thirty for a special marriage feast. The following recipes are all for a southern thali.

SAMBAR OF ARHAR DHAL

SPLIT RED GRAM

225g split red gram
½ teaspoon each of turmeric
 and salt
piece of tamarind the size of
 a lemon

THE SAMBAR MASALA:
scant tablespoon mustard seeds
1 onion, finely chopped
a pinch of fenugreek seeds
1 small cinnamon stick
3 tablespoons clarified butter
scant tablespoon small yellow
 split peas
2 teaspoons coriander seeds
2 whole red chillies, broken
2 tablespoons grated coconut
 flesh
6 curry leaves
a mixture of vegetables such as
 onions, potatoes, *katu* (white
 pumpkin), marrow, cut
 into large pieces

1 Cook the grain in water with the turmeric and salt, mash and set aside.

2 Extract the tamarind juice by soaking the tamarind in 100ml hot water for 3 minutes, then squeezing the juice into the water.

3 To make the Sambar masala, fry the mustard seeds, onion, fenugreek seeds and cinnamon in the clarified butter for 2 minutes, add the split peas and fry for 2 minutes. Add the coriander seeds, chillies and coconut and fry for a further 1 minute. Finally, add the curry leaves.

4 Add the vegetables and cook, stirring, for 3 minutes. Add the tamarind water and cook until the vegetables are soft. Stir in the mashed gram.

FRAGRANT POTATOES

900g potatoes

THE MASALA:
75ml vegetable oil
1½ teaspoons black
  mustard seeds
3 tablespoons fresh ginger,
  peeled and finely chopped
2 green chillies, seeded and
  finely sliced
1½ tablespoons ground coriander
1½ teaspoons ground turmeric
1 teaspoon paprika
675g onions, skinned and
  chopped
3 teaspoons salt
2 teaspoons lemon or lime juice
4 tablespoons chopped fresh
  coriander leaves

1 Boil the potatoes in their jackets, drain and put in cold water. Peel and cut into large chunks.

2 To make the masala, heat the oil in a heavy-bottomed pan and add the mustard seeds. When they splutter, add the ginger and chillies and fry for 2 minutes. Add the coriander, turmeric and paprika and stir.

3 Add the potato chunks and onions and fry, stirring frequently, for 10 minutes. Add the salt and 900ml hot water, cover and simmer for a further 10 minutes. Mash one or two pieces of potato to thicken the sauce, then sprinkle with lemon or lime juice and the fresh coriander.

Note: This is delicious served with a herb raita.

TAMARIND RICE

Although plain boiled rice is quite adequate, this special rice is more celebratory.

500g rice
175ml coconut or sunflower oil
5 red chillies
1 teaspoon each of black
  mustard seeds, turmeric,
  fenugreek seeds
pinch of asafetida
100ml tamarind juice, prepared
  as for Sambar (see page 23)
pinch of salt
1 tablespoon each of coriander
  seeds, sesame seeds, cashew
  nuts, peanuts and cooked
  chickpeas
a few curry leaves
1 tablespoon coconut or
  sunflower oil

1 Boil the rice until it is three quarters cooked. Drain and spread over a plate. Sprinkle over half of the oil and leave to cool.

2 Heat the rest of the oil in a frying pan. Add the chillies, mustard seeds, turmeric, fenugreek seeds and asafetida. Then add the tamarind juice and a pinch of salt, and cook until thick. Cool.

3 Dry-roast and grind the coriander and sesame seeds, then sprinkle over the rice.

4 Fry the cashews, peanuts and chickpeas for a few minutes and mix into the rice.

5 Fry the curry leaves and add to the rice along with the spice mixture and the remaining tablespoon of (hot) oil. Mix well, cover and place in a preheated 190°C/375°F/gas 5 oven for 30 minutes.

right Women decorate the street with vibrantly coloured rice powder during the Pongal Festival; Bob Kirst/Corbis

HORSE AND CATTLE FAIR

In late February the biggest and best horses, cattle, sheep, buffaloes, bulls and camels from each district of Pakistan arrive in Lahore with their keepers to attend the annual Horse and Cattle Fair. It is held in the great Fortress Stadium, just inside the Cantonment, and aims to encourage good breeding. Proud owners parade their animals round the pavilion in front of a panel of judges who award prizes of gleaming trophies and cups every day. There are stalls for equipment, trinkets and food – including Lahore's famous kebabs – and a full programme of entertainment including the unlikely feat of a camel dance.

Just as beautiful as the animals are their owners who all wear their local dress. The tall, black-bearded and fearsome Pathans from the North-west Frontier come dressed in their woollen hats and beige shawls. The Baluchis wear light colours and big white turbans, whereas the farmers from Sindh keep to their khaki tones and brighten the crowd with their bright green, red, blue and white turbans. The Punjabi farmers are the most numerous, for Lahore is the capital of the agriculturally rich Punjab. They wear a brightly bordered *dehband* – cloth which is wound round and then left to trail the ground – and exotic golden pointed shoes.

left The Horse and Cattle Fair; Corbis

LAHORE KEBABS AND CHOPS

The bazaars of Lahore are famous for their foodstalls of kebabs, chops and parathas and for their cafés clustered outside the old Mughal gates.

THE MARINADE:
50ml yogurt
½ teaspoon each of ground
   coriander and black cumin
¼ teaspoon cayenne pepper
1 teaspoon each of salt and
   garam masala (see page 17)

800g lamb cut into small cubes,
   or 6 small lamb chops
2 tablespoons oil

1 onion, sliced
1 seeded green chilli, sliced
garam masala (see page 17)
3 tablespoons chopped fresh
   coriander
lemon wedges

1 Mix together the marinade ingredients and marinate the meat for at least 1 hour.

2 For kebabs, thread the meat onto skewers, brush with oil, and cook over glowing charcoals or beneath a hot grill, turning frequently. Serve immediately with onion rings and green chillies.

3 For chops, brush with oil and cook as above. Serve sprinkled with garam masala and decorated with onion rings, chopped coriander and lemon wedges.

FRESH MINT CHUTNEY

This is quick to prepare and goes well with all grilled meats.
The quantity of each ingredient will depend on taste.

8 tablespoons mint leaves
2 green chillies, seeded
½ teaspoon each of salt
  and sugar
2 tablespoons yogurt
1 teaspoon fresh lime juice
  (if unavailable use fresh
  lemon juice)

1 Blend or grind the mint leaves, chillies, salt and sugar.
Gradually stir in the yogurt and lime juice.

Although most Indian breads are difficult to make, these are easy. They are
eaten bigger and thicker in Lahore than further down in the subcontinent.

115g each of brown and white
  wheat flour
½ teaspoon salt
1 teaspoon oil
250ml water

1 Mix the flours and salt in a bowl and make a well. Add
the oil and half of the water. Using one hand, gradually mix
to a hard dough, adding a little more water as needed.

2 Roll out a piece of the dough the size of a tangerine to
make a circle of 15–18cm diameter. Cook in a hot, dry
frying pan, adding a teaspoon of oil as it cooks on each
side. Turn until rosy brown on both sides. Repeat until you
have as many paratha as you need.

right Coloured face powder; David H. Wells/Corbis

Holi

The arrival of spring and the beginning of a new year is celebrated across northern India on the full moon at the end of February or beginning of March. For pure enjoyment and colour, it is best seen in Rajasthan.

In the days running up to Holi, housewives do their spring cleaning. On Holi eve, each community builds a great bonfire of sticks and unwanted possessions, decorating the base with coloured powder patterns. At sunset, the bonfires are lit to symbolise the end of one year and a fresh start for the next. Householders singe a bunch of fresh green lentils in the purifying flames, then eat them ceremoniously at home as the all-night celebrations begin. On Holi itself, laws and social conventions are suspended from dawn to noon. Men and women flirt, playing holi by squirting pink water at one another or throwing clouds of pink, mauve, green and saffron powder. The men sing and dance through the streets, banging the Holi rhythm out on a *chang*, a huge tambourine-shaped drum. In Jaisalmer, the walled desert city where tradition is strong, the women watch from upstairs balconies as the former maharaja continues his ancient duty and sits enthroned in the street to receive token gifts from his people – who later receive similar tokens in return.

right Students at the Visvabharati University; Deshakalyan Chowdury/AFP/ Getty Images

KHUDA KHARGOSH

STUFFED RABBIT

The traditionally fearsome Rajasthani warriors enjoy game of all kinds, from rabbit and partridge to grouse, snipe and quail.

900g–1.35kg rabbit, skinned
and dressed

THE MARINADE:
1 onion, finely sliced
100ml clarified butter
12 each of cardamom pods
and cloves
10cm cinnamon stick
½ teaspoon each of ground mace
and nutmeg
2 teaspoons hot chilli powder
1½ tablespoons ground coriander
½ teaspoon saffron, heated
and crumbled
110g dried apricots or figs,
finely chopped
scant tablespoon crushed garlic

THE STUFFING:
115g rice
1 teaspoon salt
1 tablespoon oil
450g minced lamb
1 onion, finely chopped
scant tablespoon fresh green
chilli, seeded and ground
2 tablespoons fresh ginger, peeled
and ground
110g seedless raisins
75g chopped almonds

1 For the marinade, fry the onion in the butter until dark brown and caramelised; drain on kitchen paper and pound to a paste. Blend or pound the cardamom, cloves, cinnamon, mace and nutmeg to a fine powder, then add the onions for a few seconds. Add the remaining ingredients and blend until smooth. Prick the rabbit all over and rub in the marinade, inside and out. Leave for at least 4 hours, or preferably overnight.

2 For the stuffing, boil up 150ml water, add the rice and salt and boil uncovered for 5 minutes. Cover and remove from the heat (the rice will continue to cook in its steam). In a frying-pan, heat the oil and brown the mince. Remove from the heat, add the half-cooked rice and all the other ingredients and mix.

3 Stuff and truss the rabbit, and wrap in a double layer of silver foil, crimping the edges and leaving the head open. Roast in a preheated oven, 230°C/450°F/gas 8, for 30 minutes, then turn down the heat to 190°C/375°F/gas 5 and roast for a further 90 minutes, keeping the meat propped on the pan side or on an upturned ramekin to prevent the juices running out. Serve whole or in pieces.

KITCHERA

RICE AND LENTILS

Millet, wheat and other grains that grow well in the dry Thar Desert are a staple part of the Rajasthan diet. The Mughal emperor Jehangir particularly liked this Kitchera, and ate it on his meatless days.

225g rice
225g moong dhal (yellow
  split mung beans)
150ml clarified butter
2 medium onions, finely sliced
3 teaspoons salt
pinch of ground cloves
½ teaspoon ground cardamom
1 teaspoon ground cumin
250ml milk
250ml cream
knob of butter

1 Wash the rice and beans together, then soak for 2 hours.

2 In a heavy-bottomed, ovenproof casserole, heat a little of the butter and fry the onion until golden brown, remove with a slotted spoon and drain.

3 Drain the rice and beans. Add the salt, cloves, cardamom and cumin. Fry in the remaining butter in the casserole for 10 minutes, stirring constantly so the rice absorbs the butter and turns golden brown. Add 500ml hot water and boil uncovered until it is absorbed, stirring with a fork occasionally.

4 Heat the milk and cream and add to the rice mixture. Bring to the boil, cover and cook in a preheated 190°C/375°F/gas 5 oven for 20 minutes. Before serving, add a knob of butter and, with the lid on, give the pot a good shake.

left Ricefields; David Zimmerman/Iconica/Getty Images

GANGAUR

About two weeks after Holi, this March festival is celebrated
with greatest devotion in the lake-filled Rajasthan city of
Udaipur. The long festival celebrates the goddess Gauri, better
known as Parvati. She is the wife of Shiva, one of the Hindu
Trinity, and is goddess of abundance, fertility and marital bliss.
Her name also means yellow, the colour of ripened wheat.

For eighteen days devout women dress in fine clothes and
carry water-filled bronze or brass vessels on their heads to the
Gauri-Parvati temple, singing mystical songs as they go and
then anointing the flower-bedecked goddess. During this
period, they pray for marital bliss and faithfulness, set up
painted wooden images of Gauri in their homes and eat only
vegetarian food. On the final day, the ladies wear saffron-
yellow clothes and process, singing all the way, to take the
Gauri image from her temple to a ceremonial bath in Lake
Pichola, and the image of Shiva is brought to collect his bride
in a pageant of caparisoned horses and elephants.

right Women at Lake Pichola; David Sutherland/Corbis

SOWEETA

LAMB WITH WHEAT

While the orthodox keep to vegetarian food, plenty of families descended from the warrior Rajputs of Mewar enjoy this robust meat dish.

THE MASALA:
1½ tablespoons fresh ginger, peeled and ground
scant tablespoon ground coriander
2 teaspoons salt

6 whole dried red chillies
5 onions, thinly sliced
75ml clarified butter
675g lean lamb, cut into 5cm cubes
250ml yogurt, beaten smooth
285g whole wheat grains
700ml full cream milk, heated
½ teaspoon salt
50ml clarified butter

1 To make the masala, finely blend all the ingredients.

2 Seed the chillies, then soak in a cup of hot water.

3 In a heavy-bottomed, ovenproof casserole, fry 1 of the onions in the butter until golden. Add the meat and masala, and fry for 5 minutes. Add 500ml water and boil gently, uncovered, until the liquid is absorbed. Stir in the yogurt and the remaining sliced onion, and continue cooking until the yogurt is absorbed.

4 Meanwhile, wash the wheat and boil uncovered in 700ml salted water until all the water is absorbed. Stir the wheat into the meat, pour over the heated milk, and bring to the boil. Cover tightly with foil and the saucepan lid and cook in a preheated oven, 190°C/375°F/gas 5, for 30 minutes, by which time all the liquid should be absorbed.

5 Drain the red chillies and add the salt. Sauté in the butter for 5 minutes. Serve one with each portion of meat.

LAPSI

WHEAT PUDDING

Since wheat is more readily available than rice in Rajasthan,
this is the favourite celebratory dessert.

700ml clarified butter
450g cracked wheat
1.6 litres milk, very hot
good pinch of saffron threads,
   diluted in 50ml hot water
170g sugar
110g seedless raisins
75g each of slivered almonds
   and slivered pistachios

1 In a heavy-bottomed, ovenproof casserole, heat the butter
(reserving 75ml), stir in the wheat and keep stirring until it is
toast-brown.

2 Pour in about two thirds of the almost boiling milk, stir well,
cover and cook over a medium heat until almost all the liquid
is absorbed.

3 Add the saffron and its soaking water, the remaining butter
and milk, the sugar, the raisins and half the nuts. Mix well,
bring to the boil, cover tightly with foil and lid and bake in a
preheated 190°C/375°F/gas 5 oven for 25 minutes, by
which time all the liquid should be absorbed. Garnish with
the remaining nuts.

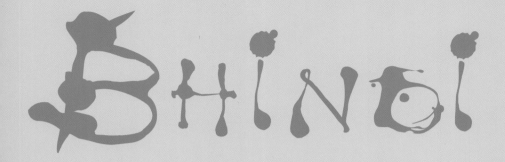

OKRA

This also works well with cauliflower florets or potatoes.

450g okra
vegetable oil
2 teaspoon ground cumin seeds
½ teaspoon each of red chilli
    powder and ground
    black pepper

1 Wash and dry the okra.

2 In a large, heavy-bottomed saucepan, heat 6–7cm of oil until a haze forms on top. Slide in the okra and fry until soft in the inside and crispy on the outside, remove with a slotted spoon and toss in the spices. Serve at once.

Navroze and Baisakhi

Springtime Kashmir enjoys a double celebration. The Muslims, who form the vast majority, celebrate the Shia festival of Navroze on the spring equinox, 20th March. The only major Muslim festival not to follow the lunar calendar, it marks the New Year in the Old Persian calendar; on this day, by tradition, the Prophet conferred the caliphate on his son-in-law, Ali. It is a time for family feasting. In Kashmir, this means ordering the great *wazwan* (royal feast) of up to seventeen courses, which is prepared by catering firms and brought to the house.

Meanwhile, Hindus throughout northern India celebrate the spring festival of Baisakhi. In Kashmir this focuses on the spectacular blossoms for which Srinagar and the surrounding countryside are famous. Fields glow with the purples and yellows of thousands of crocus flowers from which pollen is collected to make the prized saffron that perfumes and colours celebratory food. Orchards are a dreamy mass of pale pink almond, walnut, apricot, apple and pear blossoms whose nuts and fruits are an essential ingredient of the light, subtle Kashmiri dishes as well as the rich royal Mughal cuisine. On Baisakhi, both Hindu and Muslim Kashmirs throng Srinagar's lakeside terraced gardens built by the, Mughal emperors, where there is dancing in the pavilions and nightly illuminations.

right A Monastery; Angelo Cavelli/Iconica/Getty Images

DHANIYAWAL KORMA

CORIANDER KORMA

This is a favourite wazwan dish for Navroze. The fresh coriander is essential to its success.

1.35kg lamb, cubed
4 onions, finely chopped
500ml yogurt
1 teaspoon salt
½ teaspoon each of ground
   cardamom and cinnamon
2 teaspoons ground ginger
125ml clarified butter
3 garlic cloves, crushed
115g blanched almonds
125ml milk
225ml cream
8 tablespoons finely chopped
   fresh coriander leaves

1 In a casserole, mix the lamb, chopped onion, yogurt, salt, cardamom, cinnamon, ginger, clarified butter and garlic. Add water to cover. Simmer gently, half covered, until the lamb is very tender and the liquid well reduced, almost to dryness, about 1½ hours.

2 Grind the almonds in a blender, then slowly pour in the milk. Add to the meat and mix well, then add the cream and coriander. Serve with plain rice boiled with a little saffron to make it festive.

Note: This is delicious with mint and walnut chutney, made by grinding a few walnuts and mint leaves in a blender and adding some good fresh yogurt, a pinch of salt, black pepper and cayenne and, for extra spice, a chopped green chilli.

AUBERGINES WITH APPLE

THE MASALA:
½ teaspoon each of ground
   fennel seeds, turmeric,
   cayenne pepper, crushed
   garlic and salt

100ml vegetable oil
¼ teaspoon asafetida
3 large, firm eating apples,
   cored (not peeled) and cut
   into wedges
900g aubergines, sliced
   crossways

1 Combine the spices for the masala.

2 In a frying pan, heat the oil good and hot.
Add the asafetida and the apples to lightly brown
them on all sides, then remove with a slotted
spoon. Fry the aubergines in batches, adding
more oil if necessary, until lightly browned,
then drain. Return the apples, aubergines and
masala to the pan and cook on a low heat for
10 minutes, draining off excess oil and turning
gently so as not to break the pieces.

KHEER

RICE PUDDING

The nuts, saffron and kewra water lift this familiar dish into an aromatic delight, the consistency of which should be almost pourable.

1 litre full-fat milk
75g rice soaked in water for 1 hour, then drained
15g each of pistachios and skinned almonds, flaked
pinch of saffron strands
1 teaspoon kewra water (screwpine distilled essence)
250g sugar
5–6 crushed cardamom pods
4 silver leaves

1 In a heavy-bottomed pan, slowly heat the milk, rice, flaked pistachios and almonds, and the saffron dissolved in the kewra water.

2 Cook very slowly, stirring regularly – the slower the cooking, the more creamy the result. When the milk has thickened and the rice is almost cooked, add the sugar. When cooked, leave to cool slightly before adding the crushed cardamom pods. Eat warm or cool, decorated with silver leaves.

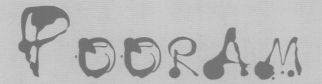

POORAM

Kerala state, bordered by the Arabian Sea and the spice-growing Nilgiri and Cardamom Hills, is distinctly different from the rest of India. And the Hindus' Pooram festival at Trichur, celebrated in April–May to honour two goddesses named Paramkavu and Thiruvambady, is like no other festival.

Although only Hindus may enter Kerala's elaborately carved wooden temples, the most spectacular parts of Pooram take place in the streets. As thousands of visitors pour in, the streets are decorated with coconut leaves, pendants and lamps, and payments are negotiated for space on rickety viewing platforms and rooftops.

On Pooram eve, thirty elephants chosen for their size and beauty of trunk, tail, ears and tusks, arrive together with their food, lorryloads of palm leaves. The next morning, they are dressed up in gold-plaited chain mail and Brahmins get up on top to hold the symbolic deity, silk parasols, whisks and peacock feather fans.

The whole party sets off on its slow, majestic, glorious day-long procession and ritual, accompanied by ear-splitting music, cheered along by the faithful who shower them with offerings of flowers and rice. After sunset, the whole procession is repeated with different music and flaming torches, ending with a massive fireworks display which lasts until dawn. Soon after, the elephants assemble for a final three hours of drumming and more fireworks.

left Great Elephant Show; Blaine Harrington III/Corbis

RED FISH CURRY

This hot dish, similar to some Goan fish dishes, is eaten by both the Hindu and Syrian Christian communities of Kerala. Housewives make it well in advance, and the spices both preserve it and improve it.

4 pieces of *kokum* (a special Kerala tamarind though ordinary tamarind will do)
1kg firm white fish
1 tablespoon black mustard seeds
1 tablespoon coconut or sunflower oil
7–8 curry leaves

THE MASALA:
2 onions
12 garlic cloves
2.5cm piece of fresh ginger, peeled
1 tablespoon chilli powder
1 teaspoon turmeric
½ teaspoon ground fenugreek seeds
½ teaspoon black pepper

1 To make the kokum (or tamarind) water, soak the kokum in 850ml water for 10 minutes, then remove it but keep the water. Then extract the juice, see page 23.

2 To make the masala, blend or grind all the ingredients together.

3 Put the fish into the reserved water from soaking the kokum. Fry the mustard seeds in the oil until they splutter. Add the masala and a little water and fry for 2 minutes. Add the curry leaves, kokum water and the kokum itself. Boil for 3–5 minutes, or more for a thicker sauce. Add the fish and bring to the boil again, then cook on a low heat for just a few minutes. Eat with brown, unhusked rice.

KACHI MORE

HEATED BUTTERMILK

This is a favourite refreshing Kerala drink, enjoyed with meals and in between. It keeps well in the fridge for several days.

THE MASALA:
1 small onion, thinly sliced
1 green chilli, thinly sliced
½ tablespoon black mustard seeds
1 tablespoon coconut or sunflower oil
½ teaspoon ground fenugreek seeds
¼ teaspoon turmeric
7–8 curry leaves

500ml yogurt
salt

1 Fry the onion, chilli and mustard seeds in the oil, keeping the heat low. Add the fenugreek, turmeric and curry leaves and cook for a further 1 minute. Do not add water unless it is sticking. Cool.

2 Beat the yogurt smooth, thinning it with a little water. Add the spices and return to an extremely low heat for 5–6 minutes to percolate the flavour through, stirring all the time. Cool and add a little salt. Keep in the fridge.

left Elephant Godhead Carving, Kerala; Harvey Lloyd/Getty Images

PAYARU THORAN

GREEN BEANS WITH COCONUT

French beans are the closest thing to the Keralan ones, but this dish can also be made with spinach, shredded cabbage, peas or carrots, as long as they are cut small for the fast cooking.

500g finely sliced French beans
2 onions, finely sliced
1 green chilli, finely sliced
⅓ teaspoon salt
1 tablespoon black mustard seeds
1 tablespoon coconut or
 vegetable oil
½ coconut, grated
½ teaspoon turmeric
1–2 red chillies, each broken
 in two

1 Combine the beans, half of the sliced onion, the chilli and salt.

2 Fry the rest of the onion and mustard seeds in the oil until the seeds splutter. Add the bean mixture, but no water. Cook on a low heat and when almost ready add the coconut, turmeric and red chillies. Cook for a further 5 minutes and serve.

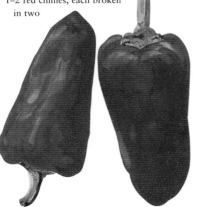

Swarantsri Pratikraman

This festival, held in August–September, is celebrated by all Jains throughout India. Jainism emerged in the sixth century, breaking away from rigid Hinduism in search of a more contemplative and spiritual life. Its leader was Mahavira, who lived as a naked ascetic for twelve years before becoming *jina*, meaning conqueror. His followers do not believe in a god but they do believe the world is infinite and that there is reincarnation and salvation. These are found through, amongst other efforts, temple building and *ahimsa*, reverence for all life. *Ahimsa* demands strict vegetarianism which includes no roots. So, with garlic, onion, potato and ginger forbidden, Jains have developed a distinctive cuisine.

Swarantsri Pratikraman is a time for meditating and repenting quietly. A week of fasting or semi-fasting to cleanse the soul is reinforced with meditation, readings from the life of Mahavira, and morning and evening worship. On the eighth day, Jains gather at their local temple or hall for the final prayers where they ask forgiveness for all living creatures of the world and for all past bad deeds. The next day there is a celebratory meal which follows the local traditional dishes but adheres to Jain restrictions. These recipes are from a Gujarat Jain family.

right Ranakapur Jain Temple; Keren Su/Corbis

The Festive Food of India and Pakistan

Puris

These fried, puffed-up breads are made slightly bigger for lunch than for supper.

115g brown wheat flour
(wholewheat is too heavy)
½ teaspoon salt
1½ tablespoons vegetable oil
+ more for frying
100ml milk

1 Put the flour in a bowl, make a well and add the salt, oil and milk. Using a hand, form a firm dough, adding a little extra water or flour as needed.

2 In a small wok, heat 4cm vegetable oil.

3 Form small balls of dough, the size of damsons, and roll out to 10cm diameter. Cook one by one, lowering each into the fat, where it puffs up immediately. Turn with a spatula, remove when golden, and build up a pile of puris on kitchen paper.

kuδi

This sweet-and-sour yogurt soup is served in a *katori* (little dish) with a teaspoon, beside the thali plate that holds vegetables, pulses, sweet, rice and a pile of puris; all best eaten with the fingers. Finish with a drink of lassi – yogurt and water, with a dash of salt and cumin powder.

THE MASALA:
½ teaspoon each of
   coriander seeds,
   fenugreek seeds,
   white cumin seeds
3 each of curry leaves
   and cloves
pinch of asafetida
250ml plain yogurt
   mixed with
   250ml water

1 tablespoon gram
   flour
1 teaspoon salt
1 teaspoon clarified
   butter
½ teaspoon ground
   fresh ginger and
   green chilli
½ tablespoon jaggery
   or brown sugar
1 teaspoon chopped
   coriander leaves

1 Combine the masala ingredients.

2 Whisk together the watered yogurt, gram flour and salt.

3 In a large saucepan, heat the butter, add the masala, fry for a few seconds and then add the yogurt mixture. Bring to a boil, stirring continuously to prevent curdling. Add the ground ginger and chilli and simmer very gently for 10–15 minutes – it will not curdle now and only needs stirring occasionally. Add the sugar, then the chopped coriander leaves and serve hot.

AUBERGINE WITH
FENUGREEK LEAVES

2 aubergines
1½ tablespoons vegetable oil
4 tablespoons chopped fresh
  fenugreek leaves, pressed
  down
1 teaspoon each of salt
  and turmeric

THE MASALA:
½ teaspoon each of black
  mustard seeds, white
  cumin seeds and ajwain
  (corum seeds)
½ teaspoon asafetida

1 Cut the aubergines into chunks and put them in water to remove any sourness.

2 In a saucepan, heat the oil, add the masala ingredients and fry for a few seconds. Add the chopped fenugreek, drained aubergines, salt and turmeric. Shake the saucepan to mix. Do not cover (or the greens turn bitter), but cook uncovered, shaking occasionally, for 15 minutes on a low heat. Add a little sugar if it is too sour for your taste.

GANPATI

In Maharashtra and Orissa, the Hindu god Ganesh is celebrated at the end of September. And in Bombay, festivities have turned from a private affair into a public jamboree.

In the ten-day run-up to Ganpati, every street corner and home has an image of the benign, fat-bellied god Ganesh. A human with an elephant's head, he is one of the most popular of the plethora of Hindu gods: his big belly symbolises the universe, his trunk is bent to remove obstacles, and he is generally associated with welcome, good fortune, wisdom and prosperity.

By Ganpati, which is on full-moon day, the city is filled with more than 6000 gaudy, pink, garlanded clay images of the god, a morsel of last year's figure kneaded into this year's clay mixture. The largest and most expensive sit on great trucks and are the results of fierce competition between factory workers; the more traditional are jazzed up with flickering multi-coloured lights or electric fountains.

The faithful put on new clothes and bangles, prepare special vegetarian food including sweet Modaks, and perform their worship. Then half the city parades their idols down to Chowpatty beach, carrying them on high or, for the big ones, in trucks. Amid clouds of pink powder, music and dancing, the images are finally immersed in the Arabian Sea and float into the late afternoon sun.

left Statue of Ganesh decorated with hibiscus flowers; Paul Seheult/Eye Ubiquitous/Corbis

STEAMED MODAKS

These are believed to be one of the sweet-loving Ganesh's favourites and are made in every Maharashtra home at Ganpati.

THE FILLING:
225g coconut flesh
225g brown sugar
pinch of salt
1 teaspoon roasted poppy seeds
½ teaspoon ground cardamom

225g rice flour mixed with
    575ml water
1½ tablespoons oil
½ teaspoon salt
clarified butter to serve

1 To make the filling, mix the coconut and sugar and heat gently. Add the salt, poppy seeds and cardamom. Mix well and cook for 5 minutes.

2 In a saucepan, heat the rice flour mixture, oil and salt, stirring until it boils, then simmer for 5 minutes. Cool slightly, then knead while it is still warm.

3 Roll two small balls of dough into circles, put 1–2 tablespoons of the sweet coconut mixture on one, place the other on top and press the edges together. Repeat until all the dough and filling are used up.

4 Steam the modaks for 10 minutes and serve hot with clarified butter.

DURGA PUJA

This autumn festival, held in September–October, is riotously celebrated in Varanasi and Calcutta. In the first, quantities of holidays and religious observances close down schools and universities for a month. In Calcutta, the three-week-long festival stops business and is rated top of all festivals in this cosmopolitan city which prides itself on celebrating twenty official festivals varying from Christmas to Id.

Durga Puja is the general name given to the autumn Navaratra, or Nine Nights. The goddess Durga, destroyer of evil, is one of many forms of Parvati, Shiva's wife, and is portrayed as multi-limbed and riding a lion. For her festival, people consecrate a round water pot in their homes, symbolising her auspicious presence throughout the festival.

But the big celebrations are in the streets. In Calcutta a community of craftsmen living in the city centre spends all year constructing and painting huge clay images of Durga, using straw and bamboo frames. On the first day of Navaratra, each is consecrated and becomes a temporary dwelling place for Durga. On the tenth night, marking the day Durga defeated her enemy the Bull Demon, the thousands of gaudy images are processed through the illuminated Calcutta streets, music throbbing through loud speakers, down to the Hooghly river. There the goddess departs from her images which, now lifeless, are ceremoniously given to the river.

left Durga Puja in New Delhi; Amit Bhargava/Corbis

ĐAI-SARSE-CHINGRI

PRAWNS WITH YOGURT AND MUSTARD SEEDS

Calcuttans use estuary prawns, known for their sweetness,
for this classic Bengal dish. This modern recipe bakes rather than fries.

450g prawns
1½ tablespoons mustard seeds,
    preferably a mixture of yellow
    and black
3 green chillies, seeded
3 tablespoons yogurt
1 teaspoon each of turmeric
    and salt
1½ tablespoons mustard or
    vegetable oil

1 Shell the prawns, slit each back and remove the black vein. Wash.

2 Grind or pound the mustard seeds and chillies with 50ml water.

3 Place the prawns and the mustard mixture with the remaining ingredients in a casserole. Cover and bake in a preheated oven, 190°C/375°F/gas 5, for 20 minutes. Serve with plain rice.

DIWALI

This is India's festival of lights, a Hindu festival celebrated in late October – early November across the country. Clay dishes filled with oil and a wick are set on the windowsills of every home, and along the balconies, rooftops and garden walls. As the sun sets, the lamps are lit and whole villages and towns, even the capital of Delhi, twinkle throughout the evening to light the way for the gods Rama and Sita to return to their north Indian home from Lanka.

The lights also welcome Lakshmi, goddess of prosperity, wealth and pleasure, for this is also the beginning of a new Hindu financial year. In preparation, houses are spring cleaned, temples whitewashed and shops offer Diwali discounts.

On Diwali day, friends give each other boxes of sweetmeats, nuts and dried fruits, and families spend the day together gobbling them up with small fried savouries such as pakoras, and drinking plenty of tea or cool lassi. In businesses, new account books are opened and, at the auspicious hour dictated by the pandits, Lakshmi is worshipped. For entertainment, there are fairs, fireworks and gambling – he who wins on Diwali will prosper in the coming year.

left Diwali Celebrations; Tom Pietrasik/Corbis

ALMOND FUDGE

Sweetmeats take a long time to make and are rarely made at home,
but you should find this simplified recipe quite easy.

300g blanched almonds
500ml full-fat milk
170g sugar
55g butter
leaves of silver to decorate

1 Grease a 20cm square biscuit tray. Grind the almonds to a fine powder.

2 In a heavy-bottomed, non-stick saucepan, boil the milk on a high heat for about 10 minutes, uncovered and stirring continuously, until it is like cream soup.

3 Reduce the heat, add the sugar and cook for 2 minutes. Add the almonds and butter and cook for a further 3 minutes, stirring vigorously and scraping the fudge off the spoon with a knife. If it has not yet reached the right consistency cook for a little longer.

4 Pour onto the greased tray, quickly flatten evenly and press the silver on top. While still warm, cut into rectangles or diamonds. The fudge keeps well in an airtight container.

CHRISTMAS

Although Christianity came to the subcontinent with St Thomas the Apostle's arrival in Kerala in the south, it was with the Raj wives that Christmas became a serious affair, particularly for children. The aim was to create everything just as it would be at home. As the author M. M. Kaye remembers: 'It was a point of honour to make it as Mrs Beeton as possible.'

In the run-up to Christmas, every household decorated a tree, bought crackers and polished up the punch bowl. The clubs staged amateur dramatics and army garrisons gave extravagant children's parties, with conjurors, magicians, puppet shows and, to top it all, Father Christmas arriving on an elephant or camel. Piles of tiny, shining tangerines filled the bazaars, while in the kitchens fresh local spices and dried fruits went into unrivalled mince pies and Christmas puddings.

On Christmas Day, the servants gave their employers trays of fruit, sweetmeats and flowers, and received in turn money, clothes and other practical gifts. For Christmas dinner, chicken and partridge stood in for turkey and was roasted plain with all the trimmings. But those on family camping trips might naughtily enjoy wild pea-hen (not the tougher peacock), which was considered sacred in many princely states and could not be eaten in town.

top right Selling Oranges on Christmas Day; Mike Hewitt/Getty Images
bottom right Christmas Eve Lanterns; Buddy Mays/Corbis

CHRISTMAS PUNCH

A pure punch contains just five ingredients – alcohol, sugar, lime juice, spice and water – since the word comes from the Hindustani meaning five. The Anglo-Indians devised their local specialities using fresh fruits and available alcohols, often exceeding the stipulated five, as this one does.

100ml each of fresh orange/
tangerine, lime/lemon and
pineapple juice
30g icing sugar
150ml each of rum and
Cointreau
2 bottles of claret
1 bottle of champagne
575ml soda water
ice

1 Mix the juices and sugar in the punch bowl, then add the rum, Cointreau and claret. At the moment of serving, add champagne, soda water and ice.

SNAP DRAGONS

Like other Victorian traditions, this was played with furious excitement in Raj India right up to Independence.

Scatter a variety of nuts, sultanas and other dried fruits on a large plate. Pour over a small glass of brandy, set it alight, and take turns to snatch the nuts and fruit from the flames.

DIZZY FRUITS

In M. M. Kaye's home this was a favourite which she and her sister Bets helped prepare each year.

In the late summer, put some prunes and dried apricots in a screwtop jar. Over the following months, add the bottle ends of gin, brandy, whisky, sherry and almost anything else except crème de menthe. By Christmas the fruits will have swollen and become very alcoholic, and the syrup is gloriously thick.

PRUNE AND CLARET MOULD

In Anglo-India any pudding set in a mould was known affectionately as 'shape'. Despite its nursery image, the rich flavour and strong colour of this one made it a sophisticated and not too sweet dish. Jennifer Brennan, brought up in India, remembers it as a favourite with the men.

450g stoned prunes
85g sugar
½ bottle of claret
1 tablespoon lemon peel
5cm cinnamon stick
1 tablespoon gelatine
2 tablespoons slivovitz
  (or any plum brandy)
30 blanched almonds
250ml thick cream, whipped,
  to serve

1 Simmer the prunes, sugar, claret, lemon peel and cinnamon with 600ml water for 20–30 minutes, until the prunes have swollen.

2 Drain off the juice, discarding the lemon peel and spice. The juice should measure 300ml; reduce it by boiling if necessary. Purée the prunes.

3 Dissolve the gelatine in 3 tablespoons of the juice. Add the remaining juice and the slivovitz to the prunes and purée again, then add the gelatine juice. Put in a bowl and chill until turning firm. Stir in the almonds, and pour the mixture into a mould. To serve, turn out the mould onto a large platter and pipe swirls of cream all around the base. Serve the whole pudding chilled.

MUHARRAM

In Islamic communities, ten days of festivities commemorate the martyrdom of Muhammed's grandson, Iman Hussain. On the subcontinent, it is best seen in Lucknow, where the Muslims follow the Shia strain of Islam and believe that the Prophet's successor is by descent through his son-in-law, Ali.

The focus is the Great Imambara. When Muharram arrives, the otherwise low-key city becomes the stage for dramatic religious demonstration. For nine days, huge tazias – replicas of Hussain's tomb, made of silver and brass by special craftsmen and decorated with coloured tinsel and painted panels of mica – are paraded by mourning men, accompanied by drummers. To increase identification with Hussain, some men lash themselves in sorrow, while others punish themselves by being suspended from a rope whose hook is pierced through the skin on their bare backs. Less harsh are the passion plays and the readings in the mosques by the *ulemas*, religious scholars. After Muharram there is family feasting on the sophisticated, smooth old court recipes for which Lucknow is famous.

right Men Carrying Muharram Tazias; Lindsay Hebberd/Corbis

MANGO SHERBET

Cool summer drinks, known as sherbets, are still prepared in homes today when the temperatures soar in post-monsoon heat. This one is given some spike with cardamom and rose water. India's many varieties of mango include indigenous ones and others introduced by the Portuguese from South America.

10 medium-sized green mangoes
200g caster or icing sugar
6 glasses chilled milk
4 tablespoons chilled fresh cream
15 green cardamoms, skinned
  and crushed
6 tablespoons rose water
plenty of crushed ice

if possible, some silver leaves
  for decoration

1 Boil the mangoes in water for about 15 minutes, until soft enough to remove the skin and squeeze off the pulp.

2 Refrigerate the pulp for 1 hour (speed this up in the freezer, if you wish).

3 In a blender, mix the pulp with the sugar, milk, cream, cardamom, rose water and crushed ice for a few seconds. Serve in glasses, laying a silver leaf on top of the froth.

SEEKH KEBABS

800g lamb or mutton, diced
75g lamb or mutton fat
1 green chilli, seeded and finely
   chopped
2 tablespoons fresh coriander
1½ tablespoons each of ginger
   and garlic, peeled and sliced
½ teaspoon red chilli powder
3 teaspoons poppy seeds
pinch each of nutmeg
   and mace
1 teaspoon garam masala
   (see page 17)
1 egg
2 tablespoons oil

1 Mix together the meat, the fat and all spices and mince very fine.

2 Add the egg and mix well. Refrigerate for at least 30 minutes.

3 Knead the mince onto skewers and grill over glowing charcoals or under a hot grill, turning so they are evenly brown. When almost done, brush with oil and grill for a further 1 minute.

4 Serve sprinkled with an extra dash of garam masala, thinly sliced onion rings, lemon wedges and Mint Chutney (see page 32).

HALEEM

An ideal warming dish if Muharram falls in winter. One old recipe demands seven different grains; this one is more practical. But Lucknow gourmets agree that serving the Haleem is always a grand ceremony, and its elaborate garnish is essential.

450g cracked wheat
140g gram dhal (split
   yellow peas)
500ml clarified butter
1 small onion, chopped
1½ tablespoons each of fresh
   ground garlic, ginger and salt
1.35kg mutton on the bone,
   trimmed of all fat

FOR THE BOUQUET GARNI:
2 bay leaves
12 each of cloves and black
   peppercorns
2 x 5cm cinnamon sticks
2 black cardamom pods
1 teaspoon white cumin seeds

THE TEMPERING:
1 finely chopped onion fried in
   100ml clarified butter

THE GARNISH ON THE HALEEM:
1 teaspoon garam masala
   (the same ingredients as for the
   bouquet garni but omit the
   bay leaves)
1 small onion, fried golden
   in clarified butter
6 fresh mint leaves

1 Wash the wheat and dhal together, then soak for 1 hour. Tie the bouquet garni ingredients in cheesecloth.

2 In a large, heavy-bottomed casserole, melt the butter and fry the onion until golden. Add the bouquet garni and the garlic, ginger and salt. Fry, stirring, for 5 minutes. Add the meat and enough water to come 10cm higher than the mixture. Boil briskly for 5 minutes. Reduce the heat, cover and cook in a preheated oven, 190°C/375°F/gas 5, until the meat starts to fall off the bone, about 1½ hours.

3 Remove the bouquet garni. Give a good stir with a wooden spoon. If the occasion is special remove the meat bones.

4 Turn the haleem into a tureen. To temper it, swirl the sizzling hot fried onions over the haleem and cover immediately to trap the smoke. To serve, sprinkle with the haleem garnish. Surround with little bowls of garnishes – such as golden fried onions, deseeded and chopped green chillies, fresh mint leaves, wedges of lemon, spring onions, plain yogurt and garam masala – to which people help themselves.